AF211644

SASHA KEEFE

MAKE A LIVING WITH YOUR WRITING

The Essential Guide to Profitable Writing, Learn the Best Strategies on How You Can Write Your Way to Success

Descrierea CIP a Bibliotecii Naţionale a României
SASHA KEEFE
  MAKE A LIVING WITH YOUR WRITING. The Essential Guide to Profitable Writing, Learn the Best Strategies on How You Can Write Your Way to Success / Sasha Keefe – Bucharest: Editura My Ebook, 2020
  ISBN

SASHA KEEFE

MAKE A LIVING WITH YOUR WRITING
The Essential Guide to Profitable Writing, Learn the Best Strategies on How You Can Write Your Way to Success

My Ebook Publishing House
Bucharest, 2020

CONTENTS

HOW TO WRITE SUCCESSFULLY

It's no secret, most writers fail before they even put their pen to the paper. If you are here reading this article, then you already have what it takes to be successful. You've chosen a tricky road. There is plenty of frustration, distractions, and setback, but you need to push on if you are going to write successfully. Let's look at ways to write successfully.

Join Writing Groups

There are tons of great writing groups out there and they can be a real benefit to the new and experienced writer. Ideas are exchanged, help is available, and there is plenty of open dialogue. Not every writing group is for everyone. So take the time to check out several and sign up for those that feel right.

You Need the Right Ingredients

The pen and paper, or your computer are the physical ingredients and they are easy to find. What's more difficult is the emotional ingredients, the technical ingredients – the non tangible ingredients. If you are new to writing there are some excellent beginner courses online. If you aren't new to writing but you aren't quite sure how to move forward two words of advice – Just write!

The magic ingredient formula looks like this:

Passion + Clarity + Good Content + Easy to Read + Good Grammar = A Great Piece of Writing Keep Writing

Write, write, and then write some more. The more you write the better you will become as a writer, and the more successful your writing will be. If you aren't sure where you niche is, try different types of writing until you find a good fit with you and your writing.

Write articles and publish them on some of the article banks. You don't get paid, but you do get exposure, and if you will get pointers where you are falling down. Don't worry, the paid gigs will come over time, but you have to start somewhere.

Publishing articles in the article banks gives you more than practice. It gives you credibility and it helps you to network with potential clients. It's an excellent way to faster learn how to write successfully.

How to Sell Your Finished Product

If you are writing books or e-books you are going to need a market to sell your finished writing project and make money. There are plenty of marketers online, but you can also find courses and help groups that will help you to market your own materials.

There you have it – you now know how to write for success. So what are you waiting for?

HOW TO BE AN ACCOMPLISHED
CONTENT WRITER

Content writing is a good way to make a living. But to do that you will need to become good at it. A content writer gets to enjoy working from home, while at the same time have new and interesting topics to write on a regular basis. If become an accomplished content writer sounds like something you might like to do, then read on.

Look for places where you can publish your work. There are all kinds of opportunities that you can write on and publish online making money. Some sites pay you a fee for the work you do, others share the revenue they earn with you. That means the better your content the more they make and the more you make. Hubpages.com ehow.com, Examiner.com, etc are examples of sites where you can generate income from the content you create.

Learn as much as you can about the sites you choose to publish your work on. Find out what they are planning to do with your work once it is published. Analyze the type of content the site hosts and check out the demographics of the traffic to the site.

A good content writer will focus on good keywords. They will spend the necessary time researching the keywords and then generate ideas for their content that will bring targeted traffic to the size.

You will want to be organized and conscious of deadlines you will have if you are doing work for clients. There are many sites that you can find clients, and the requirements of each client will vary.

A good content writer will have the clients requested language as their language. It is seen too often where a person who writes in English when English is their second language uses words in the wrong context, improper spelling, and grammar. So make sure if the client asks for someone that's native language is English it is, or native language is Russian it is. You get the idea.

Content writing allows you to have a great deal of freedom about what you write, and it remains interesting over time. Wages vary depending on topic, experience, and client. There are many sites where you can find clients, but be warned until you have built a reputation for being a good content writer you may have to work for considerably less. Be patient – the wages will grow as you become an accomplished content writer.

BECOMING AN ACCOMPLISHED ARTICLE WRITER

Article writers are high in demand. The internet has lead to a increased need for article writers as fresh and new content is necessary for websites, blogs, newsletters, and promoting your business. The first requirement in becoming an accomplished article writers is the ability to write.

If you are able to do a little research and then create an interesting article, you can make money as an article writer. To become an accomplished article writer you need to comprehend your market, and determine where your writing skills best fit.

Professional Writers

These individuals are skilled and trained to write for news papers, magazines, and other formal publications. Professional writers are required to have a high degree of skill and knowledge, earning more than $0.10 per word. They have expertise in a specific topic and have years of experiencing with this type of writing.

SEO Writers

SEO writers are at the bottom of the quality food chain. SEO involves using particular words in a website's text to help the site rank better in the search engines for that keyword. This type of writing is focused on the search engines more than it is focused on the reader. These articles are often slapped together and are lacking in quality, may contain poor grammar, and are often written by someone whose second language is English.

Article Writers

Article writers fall right in the middle between professional writers and SEO writers. Better writers will demand rates that are higher, while those who are just developing their skills will earn significantly less. Rate will vary from around $0.02 to $0.10 depending on topic and the skill level of the writer.

Becoming an Article Writer

If you want to become an article writer you need to find clients, then you can get started. The clients can be found on a number of websites where webmasters will go to look for services, as well as various forums. Some of the most popular websites to find article writing work include Guru.com, Elance.com, and Getafreelancer.com

Once you have bid on a job and won that contract, you will need to write an article based on the criteria set out by the client. You must make sure the article is high quality, accurate, with correct spelling and grammar. Of course, all your articles must be your own writing. Plagiarism is a criminal offence. Finish your assignment, send it off to the client, and then get paid. As your skills grow and as you become recognized your business will grow.

IS YOUR DREAM TO BECOME
AN ACCOMPLISHED WRITER

Do you write? Is your dream to become an accomplished writer? Great news! You can do it! If you have a passion to write then write. If you have a passion to write fiction then write fiction. If you like to write factual material then that's what you should write. Find your niche and go with it. If you aren't sure what your niche is at this point, then explore.

There are many different types of writers and not every writer will write in all the different formats. For example, there are authors who write books or e-books; there are articles writers for magazines and the internet; there are news stories; there is content for the web; and the list goes on.

If you aren't sure what it is you like to write take the time to explore. Like anything if you set your mind to it you too can accomplish it. While having a solid background with a Degree in Journalism or English can definitely help move your career forward, it's not always necessary.

Like musicians or artists that are born naturals in their field, writers can have a natural born talent too.

Remember the only person who has control of your dreams, is you. So don't listen to others who may tell you that you can't do it or you don't have the talent to do it. Follow your heart, follow your desires, and turn that dream into a reality.

Being an accomplished writer has plenty to offer you. What a rewarding field to enter. You get to constantly express yourself and you get to reach out to a vast number of readers. The better you write the larger your following. You can change what you write on at any given minute – it's completely up to you.

If you are worried about seeing your material printed a great place to start is by writing articles and publishing them on one of the many article banks. It's free, and it offers great exposure.

Your content can be picked up and placed on one or more websites. If your article isn't up to par, the article bank will let you know where you are failing. Ezinearticles is one of the best article banks on the internet.

Don't be afraid to submit articles to magazines. You never know – your article could be picked up. That will give you excellent exposure, and you'll get paid. That's a win-win.

Try to think outside the box. Use the many resources available to you and make your dream come true.

HOW TO BE A SUCCESSFUL NEWS WRITER – JOURNALISM 101

Writing news stories is different than other types of writing. Let's have a look at how to be a successful news writer.

1. The 5 W's – All worthy news stories must include a who, what when, where, and why. Make sure you emphasize the 5 W's in your story, explaining less important aspects a little later.

2. The 1 H – Let's not forget the how In a good news story.

3. Conflict – Good stories always have conflict and so do good news stories.

4. Brevity – Readers need to know why the story matters to them and they aren't going to stick around long to find out, so make sure you tell them why early. This should be at least 25 words but no more than 40 words. It is important that this is clear and concise.

5. Specificity – News stories are for the most part a summary of events and so it is important that stay specific otherwise your news story is going to become overwhelming to the reader, and they will leave.

6. Audience – When writing your story consider what it is your reader is already aware of. If you are writing a breaking story your reader is going to know less than if you are writing a print story about something that has occurred in the past week.

7. Active Sentence Structure – The use of strong verbs will make your reading more interesting. Passive reading can be dull and the reader is likely to move on.

8. Honesty – Your writing needs to deliver what you promise it will.

Things to Avoid

1. It – the word it is highly overused. Run word find to ensure you are not overusing this one little word "it."

2. Needless Words and Phrases – Watch for redundancy. Your space in your news story is limited so don't waste it with needless words/phases. Avoid any clutter.

3. Flowery Language – This is a common mistake of new writers. Use strong nouns and verbs, and fewer adjectives and adverbs.

Media Ethics

1. Identify your sources whenever you can

2. Quote your sources accurately

3. Avoid being biased – distinguish advertising from news

4. Avoid stereotyping

5. Ensure your information is accurate

6. Do not distort the facts

7. Never plagiarize

8. Rely on the most current information and research to write your story

9. Never alter videos or photos

There you have it – these guidelines will help you to write successful news stories that will get read!

DO YOU WANT TO BE A SUCCESSFUL WRITER?

If your goal is to become a successful writer there are certain techniques and skills that you need. There are many reasons for writing – some write as a pastime with no intention of ever publishing, some write as a way to express oneself, and still others want to make money from their writing. Successful writers understand how to express themselves in a manner that allows their readers to see, feel, and engage in a multitude of ways. Let's assume you want to make a career out of writing. Let's get busy.

Are you ready to learn how to become a successful writer? Until you are a successful writer, the first thing you need to realize is that your editor doesn't care who you are. The only concern your editor has is that your writing is at the acceptable standard.

In order to achieve this standard you will need to be serious and committed in your writing. The first thing you need to do is develop your writing technique that is enlightening about the world we live in. You can achieve this worldly knowledge base by reading lots on a wide array of subjects, by observing what is happening in the world, by taking notice of people's opinions, and by analyzing attitudes of the people you meet on a daily basis.

Next you need to recognize the importance of being an expert. To become an expert writer you are going to need the help of an expert writer. Start by submitting articles to a number of article sites. They will accept or reject your article. If they reject it, they will let you know what your mistakes were. There are tons of these sites. Just do a search. Although, I do recommend using ezinearticle.com as it is considered one of the leading article banks online.

To begin with don't write in just one field. Instead try your hand at a number of different areas so you can begin to recognize where your potential lies. Never restrict yourself. Finally, have some fun and enjoy your writing experiences. Here are 5 tips to help you get started:

1. Use your life experiences to help you right
2. Put your thoughts into mini writings
3. Sharpen your observation skills
4. Always have a professional attitude

5. Write – write – and then write some more – that's how you learn

You can become a successful writer if that's really what you want to do. It's really up to you.

DO YOU HAVE WHAT IT TAKES TO BE
A SUCCESSFUL WRITER?

Writing makes the world go round – if you don't believe that just take a look around you. Everywhere you look words are being use to tell a story, describe something, show us the way, provide legal protection, provide you with news, and the list goes on. Even when you are watching television the story line is made up of words – scripts someone, somewhere, has put together.

Writers are in high demand. It's a career move that's never going to be diminished regardless of how technology changes or advances, regardless of where the future takes us – words will always be needed. If you've been thinking about a career as a writer you've likely been questioning if you have what it takes to be a successful writer.

Becoming a successful writer goes farther than just having the right education. Some people never go to university and have a natural gift for writing. Others make it through university earning a degree in Journalism or English and while they have the technical skills, they don't have the natural skills to tell the story. So do not make your decision on becoming a successful writer based on your education.

Let's begin with a tough question. Have you written anything in your life that was published? Drew attention? Told a story that others liked and engaged in? We aren't talking about paid gigs here. Just writing in general. Are you a good story teller? Do you do well at collecting facts and sharing that information with others? Take a minute to analyze your strong skill sets and your weak skill sets.

Some people are excellent fiction writers, while others are excellent journalists. Find your niche and follow it. Don't try to be all things to everyone. To have a passion in your writing that will draw readers in you need to write about things that interest you.

Finally, it's time to get your feet wet. Don't be surprised if you have a tough time getting any client projects initially. There are thousands upon thousands of people calling themselves writers from around the globe, and so potential clients tend to be cautious when hiring, especially with no track record.

One way to begin to build a portfolio is to write articles for one of the many article banks. They'll provide you with constructive criticism along the way.

Not everyone is good enough to be a professional writer, but who think they cannot be a successful writer could be, if they just believed in themselves.

BE THE WRITER YOU WERE MEANT TO BE

Have you always loved to write? Do you find yourself creating story lines all the time? Perhaps you enjoy writing factual material more than fiction? Whatever it is you like to write, now is the time for you to be the writer you were meant to be.

Sometimes writers who have the potential to become accomplished writers lose focus. While they can write like crazy, they aren't quite sure how to take it to the next level and actually begin to write for profit. It's not as difficult as you might think to go from amateur to professional writer.

Start by thinking about what type of writing you would want to do if you were writing professionally. Your choices are really vast. In fact, a writer may have more career options than any other profession. Let's look at some of the options available to you.

1. Become a journalist for a print newspaper

2. Write articles for a print magazine
3. Write print books
4. E-book writing
5. Article writing
6. Write online content
7. Write for an online newspaper
8. Write for an online magazine
9. Write press releases
10. Write contracts
11. Write academic papers
12. Sales writing
13. Technical writing
14. Blogs
15. Children's writing
16. SEO writing

That's just a few of the opportunities that await you. Many worry that they don't have the skills to move to the highly competitive online market. If you are a good writer there is a need for your skills! There are thousands upon thousands of people claiming to be writers and trying to land the available online work. However, only a small number of these individuals are actually skilled writers. If you have a talent for writing there are all kinds of opportunities for you to be the writer you were meant to be.

The hardest part for writers that make the move over to professional writers is to become established and to build a reputation for quality work. Be patient! It will come. Get your website up and running, so you can promote yourself as a writer, take advantage of social media sites such as Facebook and LinkedIn, and write some content for the article banks to help you get your name out there.

Good writers find work. In fact, good writers have an abundance of opportunities available to them. There is a demand for their services. The time has come for you to be the writer you were meant to be. Why not start now?

IS YOUR WRITING GOOD ENOUGH
TO GET PUBLISHED?

There are all kinds of published authors. When we hear the word author it conjures up visions of big thick juicy books that we can't put down, or dry boring text books that put us to sleep.

However, every writer is an author – whether they are good or bad remains to be seen. There are many writers but not all of them find their works printed.

That printing can be in the form of a printed book, a news article, a magazine article, an article published online, an e-book, etc. When your writing is interesting, engaging, and quality you will find you have readers find you, read what you have written, and even share your writings.

Today, more than any other time in history it is easy to become a published writer. No longer do you have to seek out a publishing company that's willing to risk taking on a new author, and remember every year they see thousands of manuscripts but print only a select number. Today, you can publish your own books thanks to a number of services offered online.

The same applies to journalist content in magazines and newspapers. Today you no longer have to wait for that exciting opportunity. You can start publishing your writings today at a number on online newspapers, article banks, and magazines.

But wait – that doesn't mean you are successful, because almost all of these types of publishing come with no revenue to you. Even publishing your own book does not mean you are going to make all kinds of money. There's a misconception that if you publish it – it will sell. Nothing could be further from the truth.

The truth is that anyone can publish, even those who are not great writers. It also means that great writers can publish but without the right marketing they may never sell a single book. So keep this in mind.

Before jumping into any self publishing contract, read the details thoroughly and make sure it is what you think it is. One way to self publish that costs you virtually nothing is through Amazon Kindle. It's a great place to start to become recognized as a credible author.

When you are working to become published, remember that your grammar is nearly as important as your writing. Your writing submission will be looked at for content, spelling, grammar, use of the English language, etc.

Is your writing good enough to get published? There's only one way to find out. If writing is your passion, why not try to get published and go from there?

HOW TO FIND YOUR WAY TO A SUCCESSFUL WRITING CAREER

In the last decade there has been a great deal of changes in how we conduct our writing business. And the answer is "play" a lot. Experiment with your writing in all its forms – short, long, and in-between. Writer what you really want to write and take it to the limit. Now you have to admit, that sounds like it could be fun!

Too often, writers are so uptight about getting it right that they spend day in and day out studying the market, taking notes, determining what's selling, who is doing the buying ... before long they have forgotten why they actually chose writing as a career. Writers spend a great deal of time worrying about what to write and who their big audience will be.

It's time to look outside the box, even if you do it just for a little while. If you were to play what would it look like to you? If you usually write long then try to write short. If you've never played with poetry, then now is a good time to do just that. If you are a genre writer it's time to try a different genre than the one you are comfortable with. What's the worst thing that can happen if you play?

Perhaps you have had an idea brewing around in the back of your mind for a while now. You know that idea that you just have not yet put to paper, yet it awakens you, it's there while you are out for a walk, it is ready to be awoken. Take a month or two and let it out – have some fun with it.

After you've taken on this exercise in "play," you can begin to think more about how to expand your horizons as a writer in a market that likely looks much different than when you first began writing. While things are certainly different in today's day and age you can still have a successful writing career that is rewarding and pays well. You just need to decide which direction you wish to follow with your writing career today.

Take a chance and explore the many different writing career opportunities that the modern world has to offer. Whether you are looking for writing opportunities online such as writing articles, e-books, content for websites, or writing for the new book formats like Kindle, it's exciting and refreshing. Take advantage of it all and grow your writing career. The new success is just around the corner.

BEING A SUCCESSFUL FREELANCE WRITER

If you love to writer and would like to make a career of it, we have some great news for you! You can become a successful freelance writer in just a short period of time. Freelance work is certainly the way of today. It has benefits for everyone involved.

Employers who are in need of freelance writing services for a short period of time avoid the hassles of hiring and laying off. Freelance writers control their schedules – when they are available, the type of work they choose to take on, and what rates they will charge, which can vary depending on the project.

The first step to becoming a successful freelance writer is to become established. If you have been writing prior to this you will already have built credibility. You can show potential clients your level of skill by referring to past work, whether it's writing a book, writing for a magazine, or writing for a newspaper, among many other types of writing.

However, if you have not previously worked as a writer, you have a somewhat longer road to true success and an adequate income. Start by creating a website for your freelance business so that you begin to build a presence on the internet. Of course, that's just the start and explaining how to get your site to place well is an article for another day, but there is plenty of online help.

Remember to include your website as a clickable link in all your email and correspondence, which will help to bring traffic to your website to learn more about what you do. Take advantage of social media including Facebook, Twitter, and LinkedIn, which can help you to get your name out there and network with businesses, other writers, and other freelancers in general. LinkedIn focuses on business. Facebook, allows you to set up a page for free – take advantage of this, create your page, and get busy promoting. Exchange likes with others and build a network of relevant, potential clients.

Great we've touched on a number of key areas to become a successful freelance writer, but you might be wondering about the "writing" part of the equation. The truth is either you can write or you can't regardless of the education behind you. A good writer is able to articulate well and engage the reader, and they are fluent in the language they are writing in. Remember spelling and grammar are very important too. So if you can write, it won't be long before you are making it work. If you aren't a great writer, it really won't matter what you do you will struggle.

HOW TO BECOME A GOOD CONTENT WRITER

If you are looking to earn a decent living while working at home and you are a good writer, content writing might be right for you. You'll need a computer and an internet connection. There are millions of people who think can make it as a content writer, but only a small number of writers make the grade and become accomplished content writers. You need to be prepared to make very little money in the early days. After all, you have to be prepared to establish yourself before you can make decent money.

You will also quickly learn that there are an endless number of people from other countries that will write content for pennies. To these individuals, the American currency is worth a lot so they can do work for a lot less. However, this writing is seldom good enough to be on a reputable website. It's the old saying – if it sounds too good to be true it likely is.

However, in the early days, if you are going to make it as a content writer, you are going to have to be able to bid less than these people while at the same time providing top notch quality. Don't worry, patience and you will no longer have to underbid, because your reputation will begin to follow you that you are a good content writer that is sought after. It doesn't matter how much education you have, you'll still have to build your reputation.

Initially, finding work can be a bit difficult. There are plenty of sites where you can bid on work. You can search the post to find the kind of work you are looking for. You can match your expertise to the needs of the clients. Start building a client base and it won't be long before you'll have to be turning down jobs because you are just too busy.

Being a content writer can be very rewarding. Once you are established the pay is good. You work from home and you can set your own schedule. You can take time off for a vacation, deal with a sick child, or work in your pajamas all day long.

Over time you may want to break into other areas of writing such as article writing, SEO writing, e-book writing, and the list goes on – the choices are endless. If you know that you are an excellent writing, then make no mistake the opportunities abound.

TIPS TO BECOMING A PROFESSIONAL WRITER

For you to be a successful professional writer you must be able to write in a manner that is interesting, informative, and engaging. Just as some people are naturally gifted musicians or artists, some people are naturally gifted writers. Others will have to learn how to become good writers by attending classes, workshops, or earning a degree. If you have a desire to be a professional writer but you aren't quite sure of your abilities and writing skills you can always start taking courses to work on your craft.

If you are thinking about launching your professional writing career you should know there is a lot more to it than just writing. You must be able to make proper use of the English language including grammar. You will need to keep track of your business expenses and earnings if you are working as a freelancer, and you will need to know how to find writing projects.

Must You Choose a Niche?

Having a niche isn't essential for being a successful writer in a field; however, it can be very helpful if you are trying to show your expertise in a in a particular field. If your goal is to write for a newspaper or magazine, you should know it will likely take you longer to get something published if you do not have a degree in journalism or English.

Don't give up try a number of different freelance jobs until you have a wider array of experience. There are several excellent freelance sites that you connect those looking for services with freelancers. Most of the sites have free sign up, however with the free memberships there are generally restrictions in the number of jobs you can apply for. Once you've had a chance to scope out the site, if you like it I would recommend a paid membership because this will give you availability to apply for a lot more jobs.

Should You Join a Professional Association?

Joining writing professional associations is an excellent way to connection with other professional and freelance writers. You can also find all kinds of useful advice on their sites. Take advantage of the many discussion boards and forums that are available. There's a lot of knowledge you can tap into.

You should also consider subscribing to relevant magazines such as "The Writer" that are dedicated to writers and issues commonly dealt with. All of these resources can be very helpful. Keep your eyes open for sites and subscriptions that interest you and that can help you along the road to becoming a professional writer.

WRITING CAREER OPPORTUNITIES

Have you been considering writing as a career? Are you aware of the different writing career opportunities that are available to good writers? Let's have a look at some of the things you might consider doing.

Fiction Writing

Book writing is not for everyone, but it is perfect for some. Fiction writing takes a special type of person who has a great imagination and is very creative. Fiction books have to be engaging and keep the reader not wanting to put the book down.

Technical Writing

Technical writers are high in demand and are needed in a number of areas. You must be able to be write clearly and concisely, and you must be able to be very articulate.

Non-Fiction Writing

This is a wide array of writing. It is certainly not for everyone. In fact, for the most part it can be a very dry type of writing. Much like technical writing you must be clear and concise, and you must also be an expert in the field you are writing in.

How to Writing

How to writing has become very popular in the last decade. There's a how to book for just about every thing you can image from how to use Windows to how to play golf and just about any other subject that comes to mind.

Advertising and Sales Copy Writing

Do you love writing jingles, or perhaps you are an excellent writer when it comes to creating demand, desire, and strong calls to action. Then this just might be where you belong.

Content for Websites

Content for websites requires great writing, as well as an understanding of the search engines, the online market, and search engine optimization. Content writers are in demand more now than ever before as Google and the other search engines demand more from websites if they are to place well.

Writing for TV

Whether it's a TV soap, a TV series, a talk show, or… the list goes on. Each has its own set of necessary skills. The skills you require will depend on the type of television writing you'll be doing.

Journalism

Writing as a journalist means writing news worthy stories. These could be for TV news, magazines, newspapers, online news sources, etc. This is an interesting and demanding area of work that has high expectations regarding quality, grammar, and subject.

Grant Writing

Grant writing is often overlooked by writers and yet it can be one of the most lucrative income sources around for writers. That said it is definitely a great deal of work and you must be able to be convincing for the cause you are seeking funds for.

If you like to write and consider yourself a good writer, then you have the potential to be a successful writer.

ARE YOU LOOKING TO BECOME
AN ACCOMPLISHED WRITER

Do you like to write? Do you consider yourself a good writer? Have you been wondering how you could your skills to work to earn an income? There are plenty of writing opportunities available to the writer who has great skills. In fact, you can become an accomplished writer in no time at all.

You'll need to begin by determining what type of writing you do best. Then you'll want to think about whether there's a specific topic you like to write on or whether you have an area of expertise. You can always expand into other areas of writing later. In the early days, when you are trying to establish a reputation for being an excellent writer it's best if you keep your writing to the areas where you can shine the most.

Next, you'll need to think about whether you want to work as a freelancer on your own from home, or if you want to work for someone else. If you are looking to find employment with a company with benefits as opposed to being your own boss, you are going to have to go after things in a lot different manner.

For this article, we will assume that you want to work as a freelancer. You can start to build your reputation by beginning to find work on one or more of the many freelancer websites on the net. Sites like Vworker, Guru, and Elance are just a few of the sites that offer freelancer opportunities for writers and others.

Once you have signed up you can begin to look at job postings and begin to bid. Initially you are going to have to underbid most others in order to get the opportunity to win the project.

However, as time goes by and you begin to build a reputation as an accomplished writer you'll be able to earn much more.

Writing rates online run from $0.02 to $0.10 cents a word depending on the topic, the client, and your experience. In recent years, competition has been stiff so rates have been declining.

However, there is still some excellent money to be made as an accomplished writer online.

There are tons of excellent writing forums that can help you with tips on writing online, as well as networking with other professionals in your field and potential clients. If you are a skilled writer, even if you do not have formal education, the
48

opportunities are very real. You can build your reputation as an accomplished writer.

DO YOU HAVE WHAT IT TAKES TO BECOME AN ACCOMPLISHED WRITER

Writing like any profession requires your dedication and determination to make a go of it. Whether you have a Degree in Journalism or English doesn't matter if you don't pursue your passion, anymore than if you have a degree in teaching and don't pursue your chosen career. If you don't have a college or university degree that reflects your passion, don't worry – if you are good at what you do, you will still be able to become an accomplished writer, you just might have to work a little harder to prove that you are good.

Becoming an accomplished writer in our modern world is often less about the education behind you and more about your ability to think outside the box in a field that has become highly competitive in the number of writers available, and the wages.

The internet has opened up all sorts of opportunities for all sorts writers. But the same holds true for potential clients that are looking for writers. Writers outside America will often work for far less, and while there are many excellent ones, if the client is looking for writing in English they often find themselves with a big surprise when the writer has English as a second language.

Early on, in your writing career you may actually have to write for these less than favorable wages just to establish yourself and get your writing career moving forward. Don't worry – it won't always be like this. As your skills become recognized you should have no problem earning what your worth.

There are many different areas of writing so finding your niche is important. Just as not everyone is great at writing fiction, not everyone is good at writing non-fiction. Most of us have an area in our lives that we are passionate about. Perhaps you love to travel, then writing on travel might be your niche; or maybe you're a techie person and would do great writing "how to" books.

Some people specialize in writing for the internet and write on a vast number of ever changing topics in what's more of a magazine style. Article writing is a very lucrative business for those that are good at it, and with a little patience you can prove yourself as an accomplished writer and build a strong clientele that keeps returning. If this sounds like an area that might interest you, there's plenty of information available online that can help you get started.

The key to become an accomplished writer is simply being a good writer: quality, informational writing that engages the reader and makes them want to stay is a must, along with good spelling and grammar.

If you love to write, now is a great time to get your career moving.

HOW TO BECOME AN EXCELLENT WRITER

Provocative thoughts, evocative images, racing through your mind – tension where there is no pretention – that's the secret to good writing. If you feel like you are in a rut then don't be afraid to break out and become that excellent writer you want to be.

The first thing to do is take away what Mark Twain said, We will sum it up, but in essence when you catch yourself using adjectives get rid of most of them, because they will actually weaken what you are trying to strengthen.

John Gardner said, "The abstract is seldom as effective as the concrete. ' She was distressed' is not as good as, even, 'She looked away.'"

So one of the best ways to turn yourself into an excellent writer is to avoid the use of fancy words. Instead choose to write clearly and concisely, with no unnecessary words, and no unnecessary sentences. Write so that your reader can easily

53

comprehend your message and so that you are engaging your reader. In other words, drop the "fluff."

Look for clutter within your writing and get rid of it. Watch for the overuse of certain words and toss them out. Look closely at each sentence you have written and then simplify it.

George Orwell had some great advice to live by as a writer. Orwell said, "Never use a metaphor, simile, or other figure of speech which you are used to seeing in print. Never use a long word where a short word will do. If it is possible to cut a word out, always cut it out. Never use the passive where you can use the active."

Try to use short words whenever possible, and avoid long words whenever possible. Keep your writing at a grade 7 to 8 level for the best understanding. The easier your writing is to read the more likely the reader is to stick with what you have written, and to follow you with future writings.

If you plan to be a professional writer, you'll want to evaluate both your talent and your temperament. Remember, when something you have written is rejected, it's the writing the publisher is rejecting, not you. So don't become offended, don't feel stupid, and don't feel incompetent, because if you do you will never make it as professional writer.

You should also not think that your work is worthless or of no value. It's incredible how opinions change from one editor to the next. If one editor says no then take it to another editor.

WRITING FOR SUCCESS –
BE A WINNING AUTHOR

If your passion is writing, I've got some great news for you – writing for success is something you can achieve if you put your mind to it. Of course, let's not kid ourselves – there's a little bit more to it. Let's look at how to write for success.

Quality

Expectations for writers are high – if you are going to be a successful writer, your writing quality must reflect that. Your writing needs to be easy to understand and written with clarity. If you are writing in English, then make sure that you actually write English properly.

Don't try to oversell what you are writing, and don't choose the biggest words to look impressive. Rather try to choose words that your reader will understand. Use smaller words, and aim for a Flesch Kincaid Grade Level of between 7 and 8. This means a seventh and eighth grader would understand what you wrote.

Your writing needs to be passionate and articulate. Your message needs to be clear and concise so that your reader has no problem understanding what it is you are writing about. If you are a passionate writer you will also engage your reader at a much deeper level.

What Type of Writing

There are all kinds of writers – there are fiction writers and factual writers. Within these categories are dozens of sub categories. As a writer and author you can't be a great in all areas. Find your niche and go for it. You may have one or more niches. Let's say you are a fiction writer that likes to write suspense and mystery, then that's where you should focus. Or perhaps you're an IT technological writer then focus there. You get the idea.

Grammar

You can be a great writer but unless you are using proper spelling and grammar. If you are an amazing writer but the weakest link is your spelling and grammar, then hire an editor to proof your writing, and make sure it's up to speed.

Put it all Together

You need to pull your good writing together with good spelling and grammar. Make sure to read what you've written not once but several times. How often depends on whether you've written a 500 word article or a 50,000 word book. You get the idea.

If you've written a book and hiring an editor isn't in your budget, have friend, family, or co- workers read your writing. But editors don't cost as much as you might think.

There you have it – some simple steps to help you write for success and become a winning author.

HOW TO BECOME AN ACCOMPLISHED
SEO WRITER

If you want to become an accomplished SEO writer, you will need to establish yourself as a freelancer SEO writer. A freelancer is a person for hire writing because they are passionate about it and want to make some money doing what they are passionate about.

Writing online and putting your articles in an article bank can make you a writer. However, if you do not have an audience or clients then being a good writer by itself will not be enough. If you want to be an accomplished SEO writer you will need to become a freelance SEO expert.

There is no quick formula for this. It will take you time, patience, and energy. SEO writing is about trial and error. Not to worry, we'll show you some tools that can help you significantly. There is also a great deal of information online that can help you build your SEO skills. If you are really good, you'll see the work you do appear on page one of the search engines, like Google.

SEO Optimization Tools

Let's have a look at some of the best SEO optimization tools out there to give you a hand. We'll look at three that are considered very valuable. Take your time and learn how to use them properly. It will certainly be worth it when you earn a reputation as an accomplished SEO writer.

SEO Blogger – This was originally designed for Wordpress bloggers, it has become a well used SEO tool for keyword research and analysis.

Keyword Mixer – This is an excellent website. If you take your work seriously you will want to have a look at. You put your keywords in one column and then the other keywords in the other columns. You can also use partial sentences. Click the combine button and it comes up with an excellent list of long tail keywords for you to use.

Google AdWords Keywords Tool – This is a very popular tool because it's such a powerful SEO optimizing tool. It can help in making your articles more targeted. Learn to use Google AdWords efficiently and you can ensure a high flow of relevant traffic. This is the type of traffic you need to really benefit the site.

There's no magic formula when it comes to writing good SEO content. You will learn first how to write articles that will be read, and then you will learn how to incorporate keywords for search engine optimization without creating spammy content.

MODERN DAY JOURNALISM OPPORTUNITIES

Journalism has been around forever. However, modern day journalism offers opportunities that weren't around even a decade ago. The more traditional opportunities such as writing for print still exist, but in addition there are now journalistic opportunities online. These opportunities are not only exciting, they continue to grow.

If you'd like to break out of the traditional journalism opportunities, be sure to start scouting out what's available online. There are some excellent newspapers online such as the Examiner, that not only have tons of categories to write under, they cover the globe. Find a city close to home, an area where you have expertise or would enjoy working under, and then apply. Papers like the Examiner are very authentic so be prepared for a full application process. Others include AllVoices and HubPages.

Will you get paid? While some may actually pay for the content you write, many use a revenue sharing formula, where you own a percentage of what they earn. There are many opportunities here. Take the time to explore what those may be and how they can work for you.

There are also opportunities with online magazines, and many of these pay. Some are for full time or part time positions, some are contractual, and some are volunteer. Consider where your interests lie, then seek out magazines that interest you and that are a good match for your skills.

There are other online opportunities. Press releases are in high demand and require a journalistic way of thinking and writing. This highly specialized area pays well and the competition is much less than in other areas such as article writing. You can find press release contracts on freelance for hire sites or directly on company sites. LinkedIn is also a good way to connect with potential clients.

When it comes to journalism opportunities online you need to think outside the box. There are tons of different types of writing opportunities online, and since you already have excellent writing skills you can put them to work a number of different ways such as writing content, writing articles, doing SEO content, writing e-books, doing academic work, or writing reports… and there's plenty more. Why not take some time to explore what those opportunities are and how they might fit with your skills and your expectations.

It's a brand new frontier with all kinds of new and exciting income opportunities, so don't stay stuck in the past, warp to the future and be a part of it.

Printed by Libri Plureos GmbH in Hamburg,
Germany